John Thompson's Modern Course for the Piano — Fourth Grade

CLASSICAL PIANO SOLOS

18 Original Keyboard Pieces from Baroque to Early 20th Century

COMPILED AND EDITED BY

Philip Low, Sonya Schumann, and Charmaine Siagian

ISBN 978-1-4803-4494-5

WILLIS MUSIC

EXCLUSIVELY DISTRIBUTED BY

HAL•LEONARD®
CORPORATION
7777 W. BLUEMOUND RD. P.O. BOX 13819 MILWAUKEE, WI 53213

T0050650

Visit Hal Leonard Online at
www.halleonard.com

PREFACE

A rarity among piano methods, John Thompson's *Modern Course* was authored by a successful concert artist. For this reason, the pianism found between the pages of the famous "red cover" series corresponds directly with that which is required to play authentic piano literature. A musician of the highest caliber, Thompson (1889–1963) made expert repertoire choices, integrating strong original compositions with accessible arrangements of orchestral and piano classics that perfectly represented the style characteristics of each era, resulting in well-rounded students who could approach any new piece with confidence.

The aim of the *Classical Piano Solos* series is to keep with the spirit of Thompson's repertoire selections by including an assortment of treasured pieces that are taught often and hold status as prized concert music. For example, in the 5th Grade volume are two of the most recognized C-sharp Minor pieces in existence: Beethoven's "Moonlight" sonata and the Rachmaninoff prelude, loved and adored with good reason, yet sometimes unfairly disparaged because of their popularity. (Note that this edition presents the often overwhelming final section of the Rachmaninoff in a more visually accessible layout.) In the same book is Debussy's fast, witty "Doctor Gradus ad Parnassum" and Mozart's D Minor fantasy, unfinished at the time of his death and completed by his student August Eberhard Müller. (Müller's "Lyric Etude" is included in the 1st Grade.) Earlier in the series are other oft-cherished pieces, such as Grieg's spare and wistful "Arietta" and Chopin's intense, evolving "Prelude in E Minor" (both in the 4th Grade), as well as several well-known Bartók miniatures from his 1913 method (1st, 2nd, and 3rd Grade books).

Numerous uncommon treasures were also unearthed, including "A Ghost in the Fireplace" (4th Grade) and "Once Upon a Time There was a Princess" (3rd Grade) from Theodor Kullak's *Scenes from Childhood*, composed for piano students well over a century ago. Though these pieces never quite found their way into published recordings or into the hands of master pianists, for years they provided many students with delightful lesson material as they built their pianistic skills. Other lesser-known gems include works from French composers Mélanie Bonis (*Album pour les tout-petits*, 1st and 2nd Grade) and Cécile Chaminade ("Pièce Romantique," 3rd Grade); Danish composer Ludvig Schytte's Opus 108 (1st and 2nd Grade); Russian composer Anatoly Lyadov's gorgeous, seldom-heard B Minor prelude; and English composer Samuel Coleridge-Taylor's mournful "They Will Not Lend Me a Child," based on a Southeast African folksong about a childless mother (both in the 5th Grade). Quick pieces that dazzle and motivate were intentionally included as well; for example, MacDowell's "Alla Tarantella," C.P.E. Bach's "Presto in C Minor" (both in the 3rd Grade), and Moszkowski's "Tarantelle" (4th Grade).

These authentic piano solos are offered once again in these pages, reconnecting the students of today with beautiful masterpieces from bygone eras.

Correlation with John Thompson's Modern Course. The *Classical Piano Solos* series was compiled to correlate loosely with the *Modern Course* method. The series can be used to supplement any teaching method, but holds its own as a small compendium of advancing piano literature. Worth mentioning is that all the pieces are public domain in the United States, Europe, and around the world. Consequently, no works composed or published after 1920 are included. It is highly recommended that the teacher supplement the lesson with appropriate contemporary literature, including works from outside traditional Western art music, as needed.

Leveling and Layout. Grades 1-4 have been presented in a suggested order of study and progress by approximate level of difficulty. Because of the sophistication and advanced technicality of the pieces in Grade 5, that volume is laid out chronologically, from Baroque to the early 20th Century. Page turns were always a consideration during the engraving and editing process.

Editorial Principles and Sources. When appropriate, occasional articulation, fingerings, and dynamics have been added, especially to pieces from the Baroque and early Classical eras, with the intent of better assisting the advancing performer with an accurate stylistic interpretation. (An exception are fingerings in the Bartók pieces; a few were removed for ease of study.) Urtext sources were consulted whenever available, as well as standard performing editions. The first two pieces in the 1st Grade have been slightly adapted; all other works in the series are originals composed for the keyboard/piano of the time. Compositions without designated titles have been bestowed with fresh ones.

CONTENTS

[Suggested order of study; however, it is recommended that two contrasting works be learned concurrently]

Fantasie in C Major

from *36 Fantasias for Keyboard*, TWV 33:14

Georg Philipp Telemann
1681–1767

Play half notes and quarter notes slightly detached throughout.

The Ringing Bell

(La cloche sonne), S. 238

Old French Song
Adapted by Franz Liszt
1811–1886

Scherzo in G Major

Wq. 116

Carl Philipp Emanuel Bach
1714–1788

The Ghost in the Fireplace

from *Scenes from Childhood,* Op. 81, No. 10

Theodor Kullak
1818–1882

Prelude in G Major

from *Suite in G Major,* HWV 442

George Frideric Handel
1685–1759

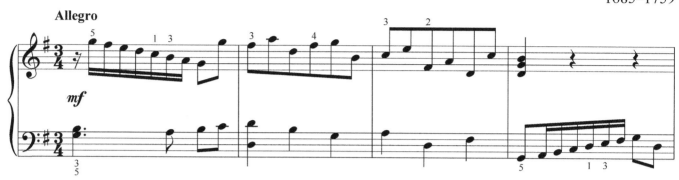

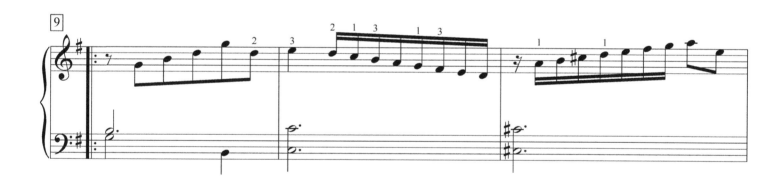

Play eighth notes and quarter notes slightly detached.

The Music Lesson

from *Tableaux pour enfants,* Op. 37, No. 2

Vladimir Rebikov
1866–1920

A student is practicing Mozart at the piano,
but is becoming increasingly distracted by the
scent of lilacs and roses out the open window...

Con entusiasmo

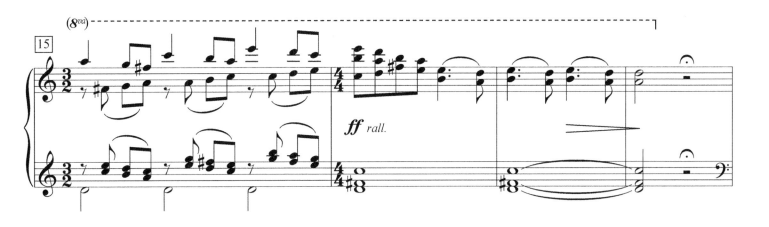

Moderato

Più mosso

...escapes to the garden.

Flying Leaves
Op. 147, No. 2

Carl Kölling
1831–1914

The Little Girls' Dance

from *Börnenes Jul,* Op. 36, No. 3

Niels Gade
1817–1890

Sonata in G Major

K. 391, L. 79, P. 364

Domenico Scarlatti
1685–1757

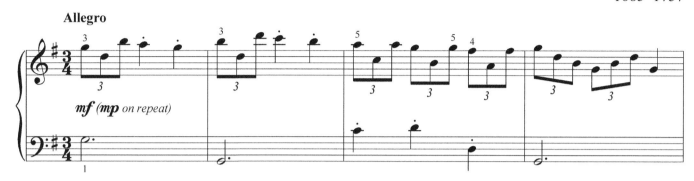

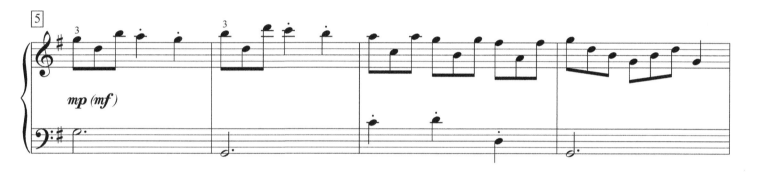

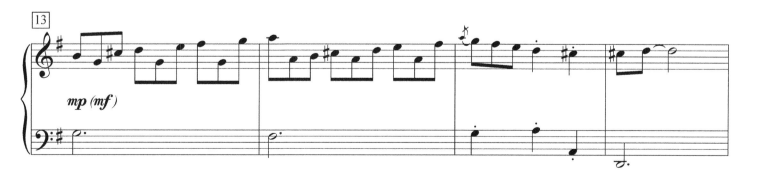

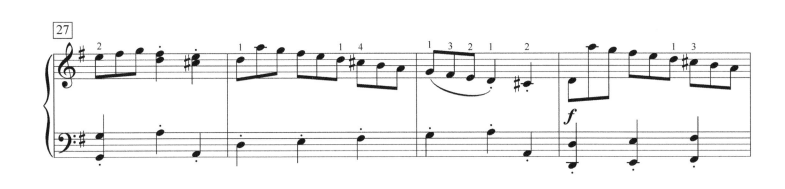

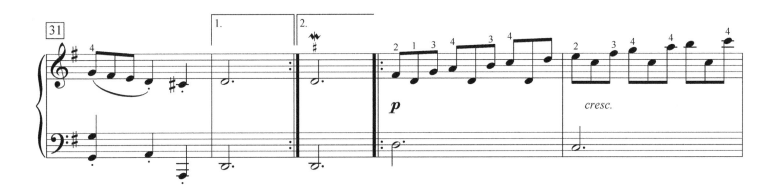

Sailor's Song

from *25 Melodious Etudes,* Op. 45, No. 14

Stephen Heller
1813–1888

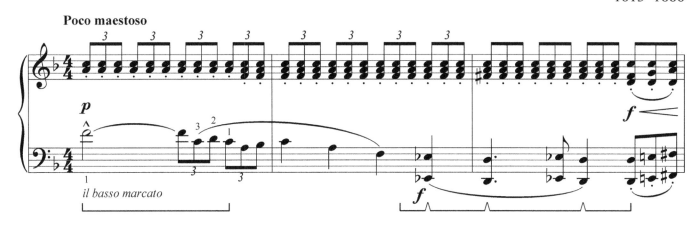

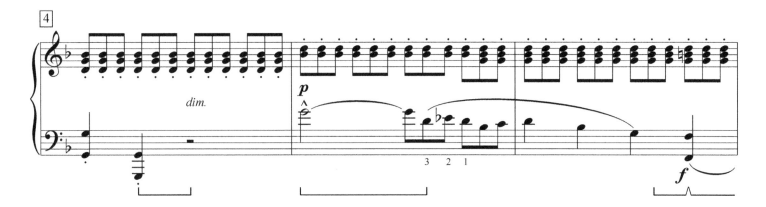

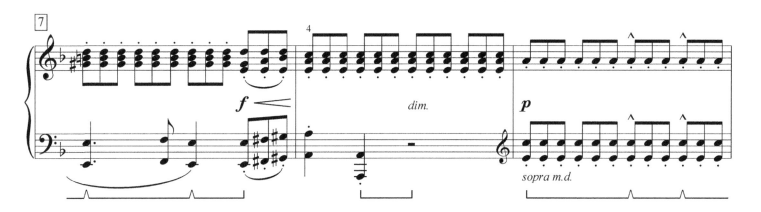

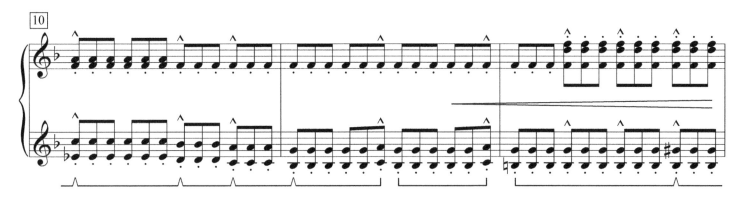

Arietta

from *Lyric Pieces,* Op. 12, No. 1

Edvard Grieg
1843–1907

Poco andante e sostenuto

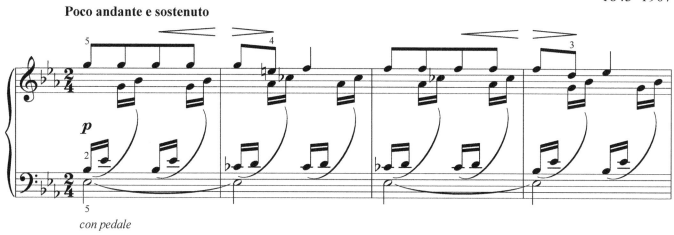

con pedale

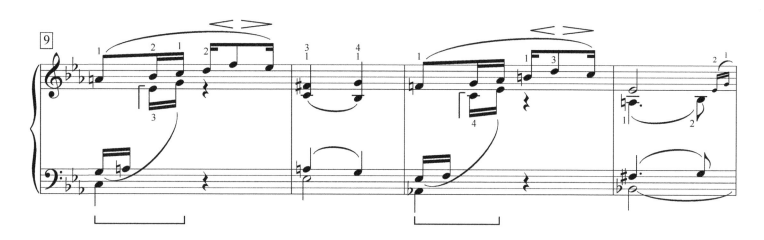

Sonatina in C Major
Op. 20, No. 1

Friedrich Kuhlau
1786–1832

I. Allegro

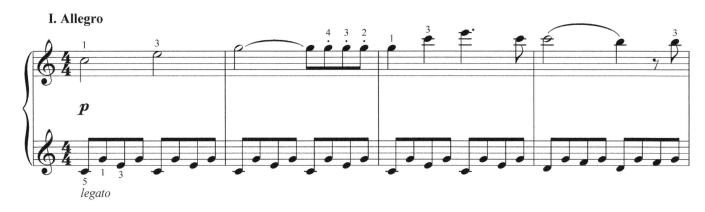

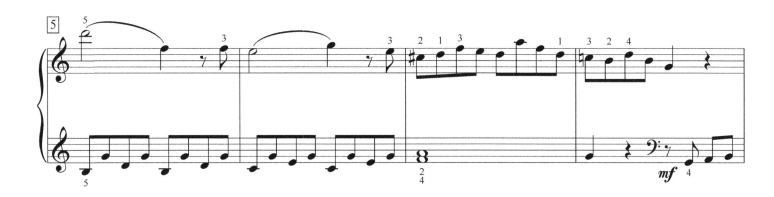

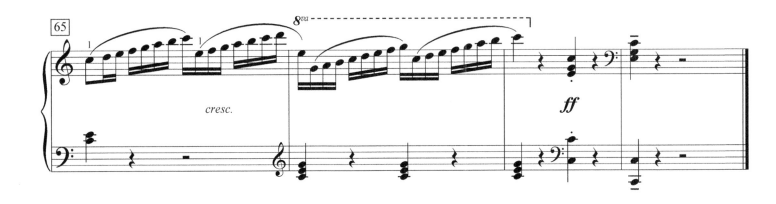

II. Andante

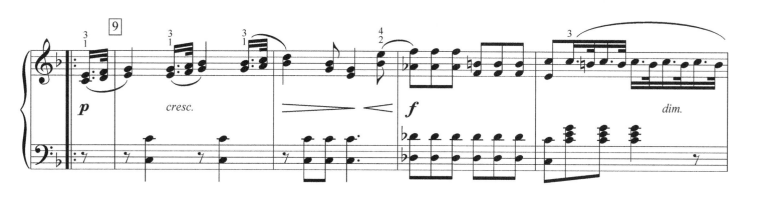

III. RONDO: Allegro

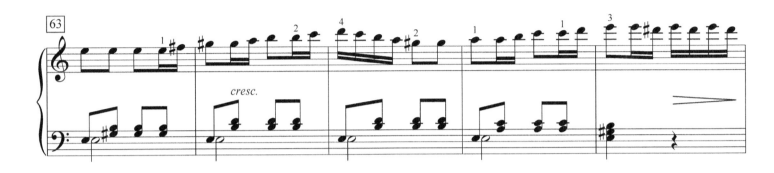

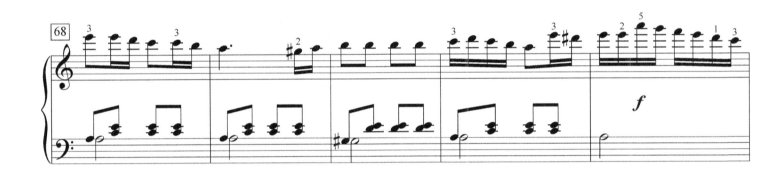

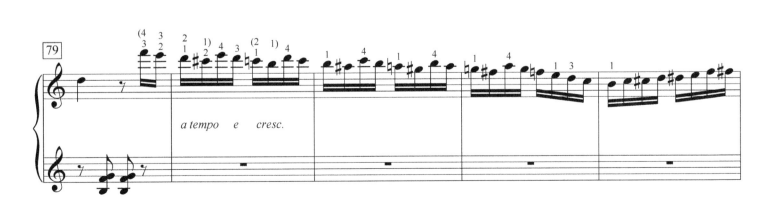

Prelude in E Minor
Op. 28, No. 4

Frédéric Chopin
1810–1849

Largo

* con pedale

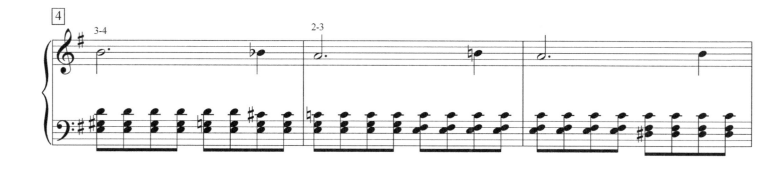

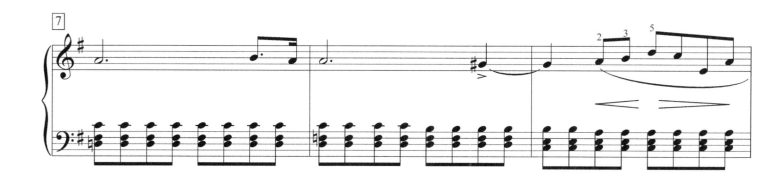

* change pedal at each harmonic shift

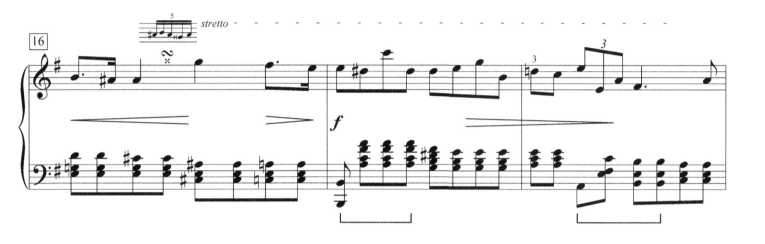

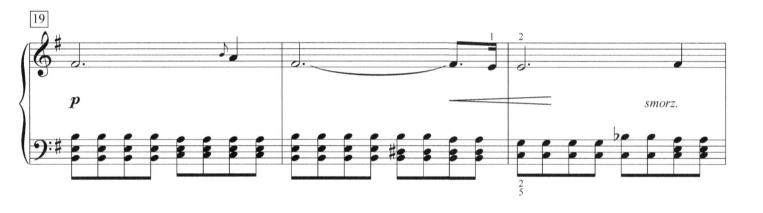

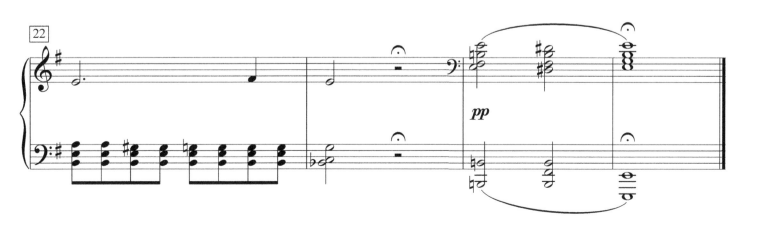

Berceuse
(Le sommeil de l'enfant) Op. 35

A mon père

Teresa Carreño
1853–1917

46

Allegro in G Minor

from *The London Notebook,* KV 15p (K. Anh. 109b No. 3)

Wolfgang Amadeus Mozart
1756–1791

Play eighth notes slightly detached.

Valse Poetic No. 6

from *8 Valses Poeticos*

Enrique Granados
1867–1916

Quasi ad libitum

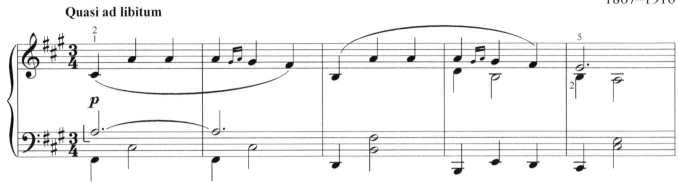

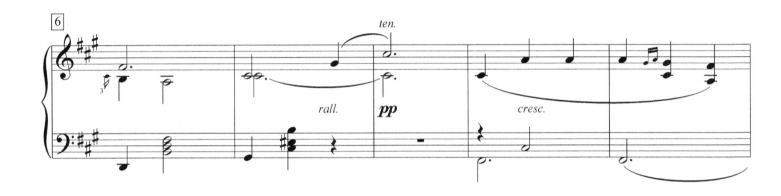

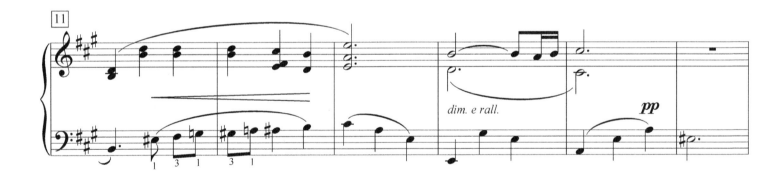

Tarantelle
from *10 Pièces mignonnes,* Op. 77, No. 6

Moritz Moszkowski
1854–1925

Gymnopédie No. 1

from *Trois Gymnopédies*

à Mademoiselle Jeanne de Bret

Erik Satie
1866–1925

* Slow and painful.

Style characteristics and adjectives that may be helpful when teaching Western keyboard classical music:

BAROQUE (c. 1600-1750) – ornamented, verbose, grand, delicate, decorative, propulsive, embellished, improvisatory, speech-like inflections, counterpoint, binary form, motoric rhythms, drive to the last note of a phrase, the idea of "affections" (each piece has single mood/character).
Major Keyboard Composers: Bach, Handel, Rameau, Scarlatti.

CLASSICAL (c. 1750-1820) – simple, elegant, graceful, natural, melodic, pure, precise, balanced, homophonic (melody with accompaniment), Alberti bass, sonata form, tapered phrases, symmetrical phrases, motivic development, contrasting moods, grace notes played on the beat.
Major Keyboard Composers: Beethoven, Haydn, Mozart.

ROMANTIC (c. 1800-1910) – emotional, dramatic, melodic, *sturm und drang*, flexible, expressive, personal, chromatic, virtuosic, forlorn, nationalistic, programmatic, singing melodies, long gestures, wide leaps, modulations to remote keys, character pieces.
Major Keyboard Composers: Brahms, Chopin, Grieg, Liszt, Mendelssohn, Rachmaninoff, Schumann, Scriabin.

IMPRESSIONIST (c. 1875-1925) – blurry, hazy, misty, colorful, ambiguous (tonality), evocative, parallel chords (planing), pentatonic and whole-tone scales, irregular meter, small/repeated motives and phrases, poetry, painting, nature, mood over clarity, extreme ranges of pitch and dynamics.
Major Keyboard Composers: Debussy, Ravel.

20th CENTURY / CONTEMPORARY (c. 1900-present) – experimental, percussive, complex, electronic, dissonant, atonal, asymmetrical rhythms, changing meters, twelve-tone, serialism, eclectic, diverse formal structures, specific performing directions, individual, folk melodies, global influences.
Major Keyboard Composers: Bartók, Prokofiev.

PHILIP LOW is a piano teacher in Arden Hills, Minnesota, where he maintains a private studio of nearly 50 students. His students have won numerous competitions, including the MMTA state, Young Artist, Northstar Concerto, Piano Fun, and Saint Paul Piano Teachers contests. An active member of MMTA, Dr. Low has volunteered on the convention committee, exam syllabus committee, and foundation board. He has given lectures at the state convention as well as to local music teacher groups. He holds a Masters and Doctorate in piano performance from the Cleveland Institute of Music as well as a Bachelor of Music from Bethel University in St. Paul.

SONYA SCHUMANN received her D.M.A. and M.M. in piano performance and pedagogy from the University of Michigan and a B.M. from the University of South Carolina. She has performed throughout the United States, Canada, Europe, and Australia, and with orchestras across North America, winning top prizes in several competitions. Active in the artistic community, she also serves as an ambassador for the Piano Arts Consortium, performing benefit concerts and giving masterclasses across the East Coast. She has appeared as guest lecturer and masterclass presenter at several festivals and colleges, including Keys Fest, Music Teachers National Association, Central Michigan University, Red Rocks Music Festival, and Art at Noon at LexArts. She has served as faculty at Madonna University and Schoolcraft College. Dr. Schumann has been on the Levine Music School faculty since 2015, teaching group piano classes and private piano.

CHARMAINE SIAGIAN is editor of Willis publications at Hal Leonard Corporation. She received her D.M.A. in piano performance and pedagogy from the University of Oklahoma and her B.M. and M.M. in piano performance from the Dana School of Music at Youngstown State University. Dr. Siagian has served on the piano faculties of Youngstown State University and Mid-America Christian University, teaching classes in applied and group piano, music theory and history, as well as accompanying chamber choirs, musical theater, and opera workshops. Growing up on North Borneo, her first piano book—perhaps fortuitously—was by John Thompson.

CLASSIC PIANO REPERTOIRE
from Willis Music

The *Classic Piano Repertoire* series includes popular as well as lesser-known pieces from a select group of composers out of the Willis piano archives. Every piece has been newly engraved and edited with the aim to preserve each composer's original intent and musical purpose.

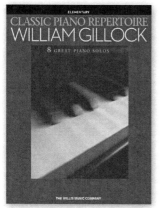

WILLIAM GILLOCK - ELEMENTARY LEVEL
8 Great Piano Solos

Dance in Ancient Style • Little Flower Girl of Paris • On a Paris Boulevard • Rocking Chair Blues • Sliding in the Snow • Spooky Footsteps • A Stately Sarabande • Stormy Weather.

00416957 ....$8.99

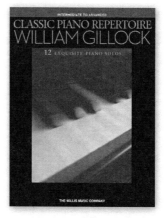

WILLIAM GILLOCK - INTERMEDIATE TO ADVANCED LEVEL
12 Exquisite Piano Solos

Classic Carnival • Etude in A Major (The Coral Sea) • Etude in E Minor • Etude in G Major (Toboggan Ride) • Festive Piece • A Memory of Vienna • Nocturne • Polynesian Nocturne • Sonatina in Classic Style • Sonatine • Sunset • Valse Etude.

00416912 .... $12.99

EDNA MAE BURNAM - ELEMENTARY LEVEL
8 Great Piano Solos

The Clock That Stopped • The Friendly Spider • A Haunted House • New Shoes • The Ride of Paul Revere • The Singing Cello • The Singing Mermaid • Two Birds in a Tree.

00110228 ....$8.99

EDNA MAE BURNAM - INTERMEDIATE TO ADVANCED LEVEL
13 Memorable Piano Solos

Butterfly Time • Echoes of Gypsies • Hawaiian Leis • Jubilee! • Longing for Scotland • Lovely Senorita • The Mighty Amazon River • Rumbling Rumba • The Singing Fountain • Song of the Prairie • Storm in the Night • Tempo Tarantelle • The White Cliffs of Dover.

00110229 .... $12.99

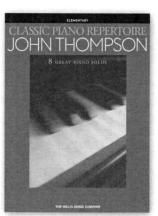

JOHN THOMPSON - ELEMENTARY LEVEL
9 Great Piano Solos

Captain Kidd • Drowsy Moon • Dutch Dance • Forest Dawn • Humoresque • Southern Shuffle • Tiptoe • Toy Ships • Up in the Air.

00111968 ....$8.99

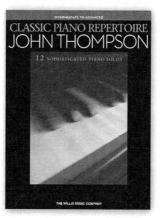

JOHN THOMPSON - INTERMEDIATE TO ADVANCED LEVEL
12 Masterful Piano Solos

Andantino (from Concerto in D Minor) • The Coquette • The Faun • The Juggler • Lagoon • Lofty Peaks • Nocturne • Rhapsody Hongroise • Scherzando in G Major • Tango Carioca • Valse Burlesque • Valse Chromatique.

00111969 .... $12.99